HIDDEN DINOSAURS

First Edition

Library of Congress Cataloging-in-Publication Data

Kchodl, Joseph J.
  Hidden dinosaurs / written by Joseph J. Kchodl, illustrated by
Jim DeWildt. -- 1st ed.
     p. cm.
  ISBN-13: 978-1-934133-00-2 (hardcover : alk. paper)
  ISBN-10: 1-934133-00-0 (hardcover : alk. paper)
 1. Dinosaurs--Juvenile literature. 2. Vertebrates, Fossil--Juvenile
literature. I. DeWildt, Jim, 1950- ill. II. Title.
QE861.5.K35 2006
567.9--dc22
                           2006023856

Summary: Hidden Dinosaurs is a fun-filled dinosaur hunting and fossil collecting
hide and seek book, filled with dinosaur rhymes and interesting dinosaur facts.

Non-Fiction
10 9 8 7 6 5 4 3 2 1

Printed and bound in Canada by Friesens, Altona, Manitoba.

A Mackinac Island Press, Inc. publication
Traverse City, Michigan

www.mackinacislandpress.com

To children everywhere who question, ask, and learn.

Joseph J. "PaleoJoe" Kchodl

To my beautiful wife Manie,
for all her love and support.

Jim DeWildt

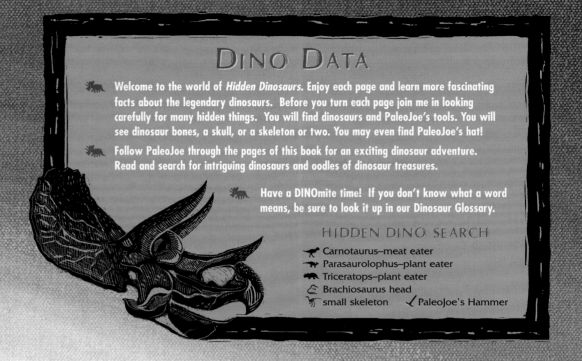

Big dinosaurs, small dinosaurs,
dinosaurs of every type.
Dinosaurs eating, dinosaurs sleeping,
or fiercely fighting for their life.

Dinosaurs with great big humps
and some with many spikes.
Dinosaurs with speckled spots
or even silly stripes.

Plant eating and meat eating dinosaurs
hunting food for their dinosaur clan.
Dinosaurs from long ago
left their footprints in the sand.

My name is PaleoJoe;
come explore and search with me.
We'll look for big fierce dinosaurs,
for their bones and big sharp teeth.

We're going on a dino dig,
hunting for bones across the land.
We'll hunt them under every stone,
in the dirt and rock and sand.

Be careful where you look,
and be careful where you stand.
You may be in a T rex mouth,
with his slimy saliva gland.

DINO DATA

- A Paleontologist—like PaleoJoe—studies fossils.
- Fossils are the remains of plants and animals that died millions of years ago or the evidence that such life existed, such as footprints or other traces.
- Many paleontologists are "diggers" searching the world for dinosaur bones and other fossils.
- Fossils are normally found in sedimentary rock. They are not found in igneous or volcanic rock and only very rarely in metamorphic rock.

HIDDEN DINO SEARCH

Compsognathus–meat eater   Ankylosaurus–plant eater   Brachiosaurus–plant eater

Tyrannosaurus Rex tooth   Triceratops skull   volcano

DINO DATA

- Fossils can be the actual bones or remains of prehistoric creatures.
- Dinosaurs lived from the Triassic period 245 million years ago to approximately 65 million years ago at the end of the Cretaceous period.
- Trace fossils are another form of detailed evidence that something existed at one time. Trace fossils might include track marks like dinosaur footprints or coprolites--fossilized feces or dino poop, or rhizoliths--fossil remains of roots of plants. Remember the evidence is in the details.

HIDDEN DINO SEARCH

Deinonychus–meat eater   Pachycephalosaurus–plant eater   Centrosaurus–plant eater

wisk broom   notebook   pencil

Fossils are evidence of life in the past—
over a million years old, now you do the math.

Fossils are remains of dino bones
and even some big leafy plants.
They are also insects that lived in the past—
some even as small as ants.

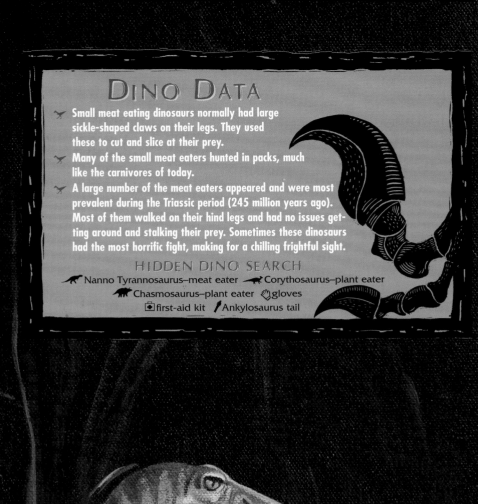

Some meat eaters were big and stood very, very tall:
Allosaurus, Carnotaurus, T rex and all.

Some meat eaters were small and really quite fast:
Coelophysis, Deinonychus, and many more from the past.

They ran quick on two legs to catch their prey,
eating many different dinosaurs all night and all day.

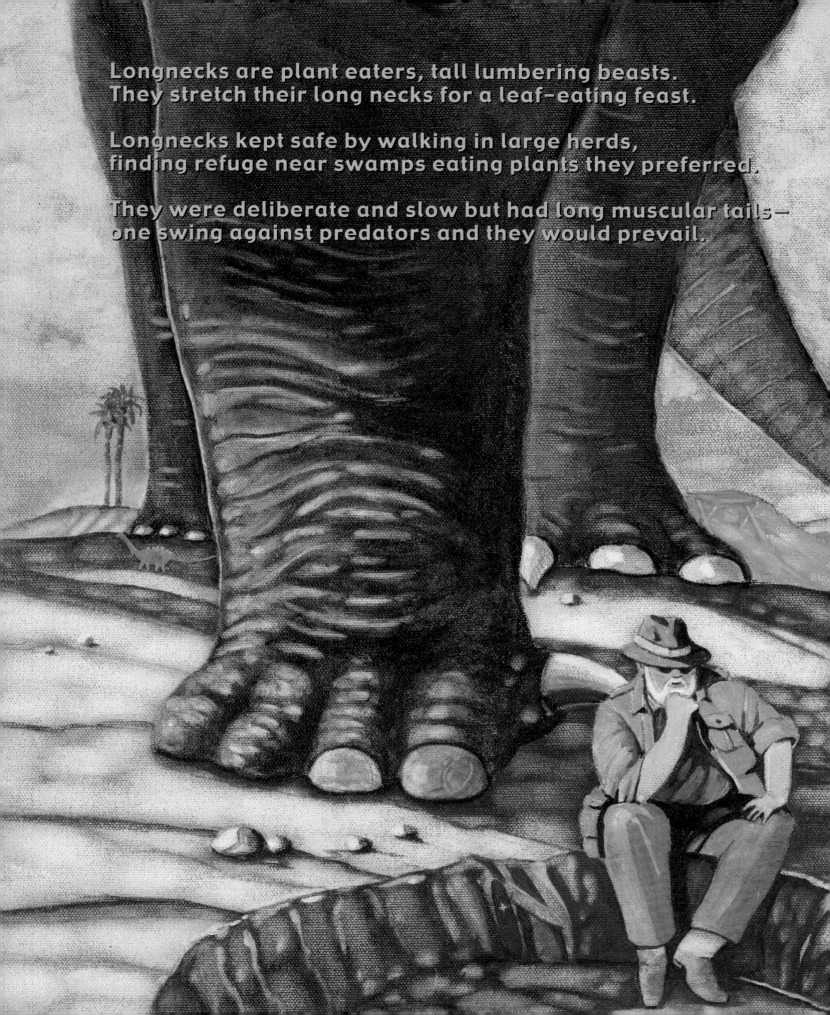

Longnecks are plant eaters, tall lumbering beasts.
They stretch their long necks for a leaf-eating feast.

Longnecks kept safe by walking in large herds,
finding refuge near swamps eating plants they preferred.

They were deliberate and slow but had long muscular tails—
one swing against predators and they would prevail.

DINO DATA

- Longnecks began to appear during the late Triassic period (245-200 million years ago).
- Longneck dinosaurs were herbivores—meaning they ate plants. They had long necks to reach high into the trees to get the new and tender leaves and branches. They had long and muscular tails they used as whips to keep danger away.
- Take a look at your neck. Are you a longneck too?

HIDDEN DINO SEARCH

Camarasaurus–plant eater   Saltasaurus–plant eater   Siesmosaurus–plant eater

camera   centipede   jeep

Do you think our old dino friends ever got wet?
Just like today's swimming sea creatures...you bet!

What about food? Like the water animals of today
water dinos ate smaller sea creatures as their prey.

The dolphin resembles the prehistoric Ichthyosaur,
a strong dino swimmer no doubt,
with its long muscular tail swishing around
and its long pointed dinosaur snout.

DINO DATA

- A *Plesiosaur* was a fast swimmer that had four paddle-like legs that made him very swift and agile.
- Most of the aquatic dinosaurs had rows of very large and sharp teeth they used to catch their prey. Their teeth would grow one below another, and as one would break off during feeding another stood ready to grow and take its place, just like sharks.
- The largest species of aquatic dinosaurs, the *Mosasaurus*, was about the size of the whale.

HIDDEN DINO SEARCH

Mosasaurus–meat eater   Ichthyosaurus–meat eater   Plesiosaur–meat eater   backpack   trowel   raptor claw

DINO DATA

Some dinosaurs had hard external body plates they used as protection from danger.

Triceratops, Stegosaurus, and dinosaurs called Hadrosaurs were a few plant eaters that were very large. The Hadrosaurs were also called duck-billed dinosaurs. They all ate lots of vegetation: they were herbivores. They had large heavy tails for use as a counterbalance when walking on all fours. The young of duck-billed dinosaurs grew very fast. They could grow to adult size in as little as four years.

Each duck-bill had a different way of protecting itself. We believe most of the duck-bills that had crests on their heads, used the nasal passages and hollows of the crests as bullhorns, sounding out when danger came around. They also traveled in herds for protection.

Triceratops were similar to the rhinos of Africa today. They were herbivores and plant eaters that had a unique form of defense, an obvious form of defense. Utilizing his three horns, the *Triceratops* could stab at any enemy, and by using his giant neck frill he could protect the back of his head from attack.

HIDDEN DINO SEARCH

Coelophysis–meat eater   Psittacosaurus–plant eater

Diplodocus–plant eater   suntan lotion

microscope   trilobite

Plant eaters ate healthy, but were really quite slow,
some had protective bodies to keep them safe from tough blows.

Some plant eaters were armed with large horns and big spikes—
like the 30 foot Triceratops—he was no tiny tike!

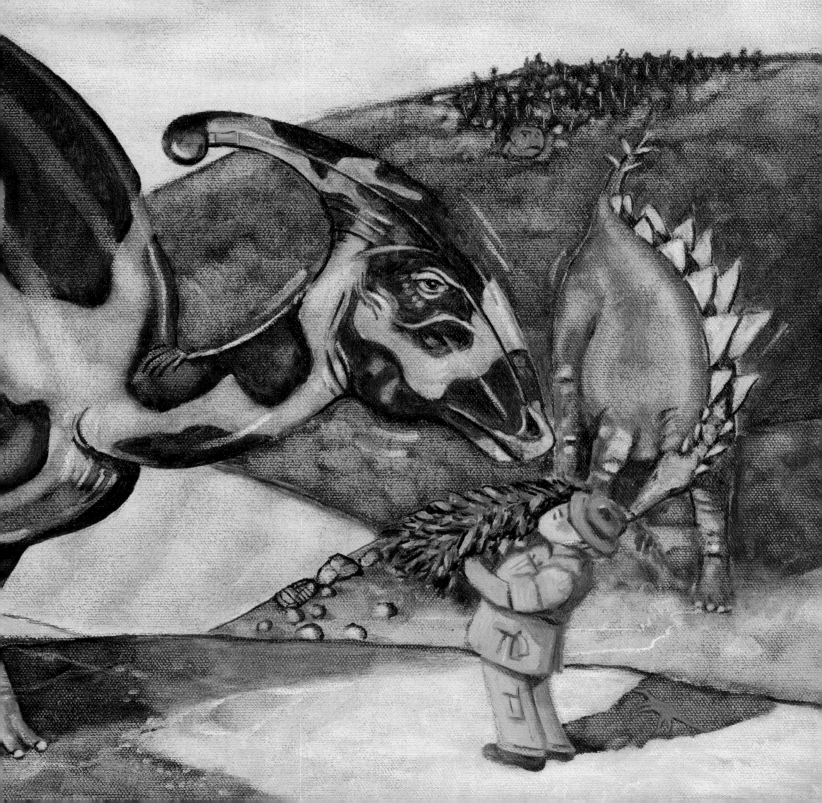

Now, what about our flying fossil friends
soaring through the air?
Some swoop to the water to catch their prey,
and escape without a care.

Here is a question for you—

What about dinosaurs and birds?
Is there a missing link?
It's the flying dinosaur with feathers,
some paleontologists think.

DINO DATA

🦅 Some dinosaurs were found with primitive feathers that look like hollow quills, or downy feathers like those found on baby birds. Some feathers were short and stubbly. Impressions of fossil feathers were found intact. Though many dinosaurs couldn't fly, some did have feathers to keep them warm and dry.

🦅 *Pterosaurs* were actually flying reptiles. Though they could fly, they were not related to birds. *Pterosaurs* were graceful and swift flyers but had no feathers.

🦅 *Archaeopteryx* was a feathered dinosaur that was able to fly with his primitive feathers.

🦅 Today paleontologists believe that many of the small theropod dinosaurs that couldn't fly actually did have primitive feathers.

🦅 Bird-like dinosaurs began to appear during the Jurassic period (200-145 million years ago). Long and sleek, they swirled and swooped and turned like fighter planes.

HIDDEN DINO SEARCH

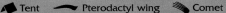 Archaeopteryx–meat eater 　— Pteranodon–meat eater 　 Sinosauropteryx–meat eater

🔺 Tent 　— Pterodactyl wing 　＼ Comet

The Stegosaurus—so slow, short, and stout,
had grinding teeth in his long pointed snout.
He has big long spikes for defense and display
at the end of his tail to keep danger away.

We now know solar science existed before us,
Because of the sun-soaking plates on the great Stegosaurus.

DINO DATA

- Plant eating dinosaurs are called herbivores. Plant eaters would eat plants such as ferns, tree twigs, and leaves.
- Some plant eating dinosaurs had peg-like teeth. Some had flat grinding teeth.
- Plant eaters were generally very slow. Because of their large, massive size most plant eaters moved slowly to conserve energy. They walked along on all fours and traveled in large herds.
- Because they were the food for meat eaters, they had varied forms of defense and armor.
- The Stegosaurus possessed plates along its back for soaking up the sun to heat his body—thermal heating. Solar science existed some 140 million years ago, during the Cretaceous period.

HIDDEN DINO SEARCH

Tyrannosaurus Rex–meat eater   Stegosaurus–plant eater

Iguanodon–plant eater   Stegosaurus skull

piece of amber with a bug in it   a magnifying glass

Some dinosaur eggs are bumpy and round.
Travel off to China where the best nests are found.

Don't snatch an egg from a dinosaur's nest,
or a mother dinosaur will most likely protest!

To dig for dinosaurs and break them free,
there are many special tools you are going to need.

Shovels and sieves chip away...tick, tick.
Hammers and chisels and big heavy picks.

A hat and some water and a good pair of shoes,
safety goggles and gloves are other tools you will use .

DINO DATA

- Most dinosaur bone collecting is done with small tools because dinosaur bones, though sometimes large, can be very delicate.
- Paint brushes help brush away the dust and dirt to help paleontologists find the bones.
- Small hammers and chisels are used to free the bones from the sedimentary rock. Some fossils can be found in sediments as soft as sand.

HIDDEN DINO SEARCH

Velociraptor–meat eater   Protoceratops–plant eater
Oviraptor–plant eaters   raptor skull
PaleoJoe's hat   large dinosaur footprint

Dinosaurs stomped around the land,
leaving many dino footprints in the sand.

We call these footprints a fossil trace,
showing dinosaurs moved from place to place.

Dinosaur trackways show how fast they moved.
Did they move one by one or two by two?

DINO DATA

Dinosaur footprints tell us more about dinosaurs than mere bones can. They can tell us about their behavior and if they moved in herds or if they were more solitary. They reveal what kind of dinosaurs lived so many years ago.

By using mathematical formulas we can tell how fast dinosaurs moved just by measuring their footprint stride and pace along with the length of the leg.

Their tracks tell us many dinosaur stories of triumphs and even their many battles.

Trackways have been found on continents worldwide and also right here in the United States in places such as Wyoming, Arizona, and Texas.

HIDDEN DINO SEARCH

Albertosaurus–meat eater   Styracosaurus–plant eater
Gallimimus–plant eater   footprints
map   giant dragonfly

Meet Dinosaur Sue with her razor-sharp teeth—
she is massive yet graceful with her bird-like feet.

Running next to Sue is her young friend Jane.
Both built for speed they would never be tame.

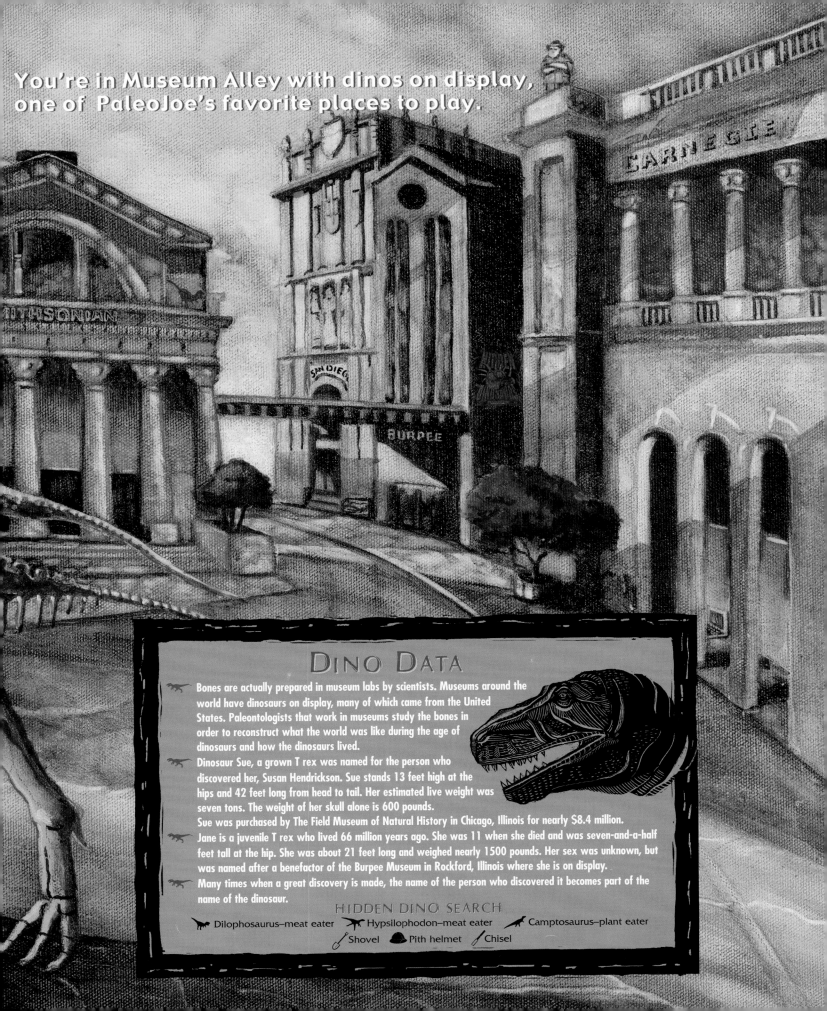

You're in Museum Alley with dinos on display,
one of PaleoJoe's favorite places to play.

DINO DATA

Bones are actually prepared in museum labs by scientists. Museums around the world have dinosaurs on display, many of which came from the United States. Paleontologists that work in museums study the bones in order to reconstruct what the world was like during the age of dinosaurs and how the dinosaurs lived.

Dinosaur Sue, a grown T rex was named for the person who discovered her, Susan Hendrickson. Sue stands 13 feet high at the hips and 42 feet long from head to tail. Her estimated live weight was seven tons. The weight of her skull alone is 600 pounds.

Sue was purchased by The Field Museum of Natural History in Chicago, Illinois for nearly $8.4 million.

Jane is a juvenile T rex who lived 66 million years ago. She was 11 when she died and was seven-and-a-half feet tall at the hip. She was about 21 feet long and weighed nearly 1500 pounds. Her sex was unknown, but was named after a benefactor of the Burpee Museum in Rockford, Illinois where she is on display.

Many times when a great discovery is made, the name of the person who discovered it becomes part of the name of the dinosaur.

HIDDEN DINO SEARCH

Dilophosaurus—meat eater   Hypsilophodon—meat eater   Camptosaurus—plant eater

Shovel   Pith helmet   Chisel

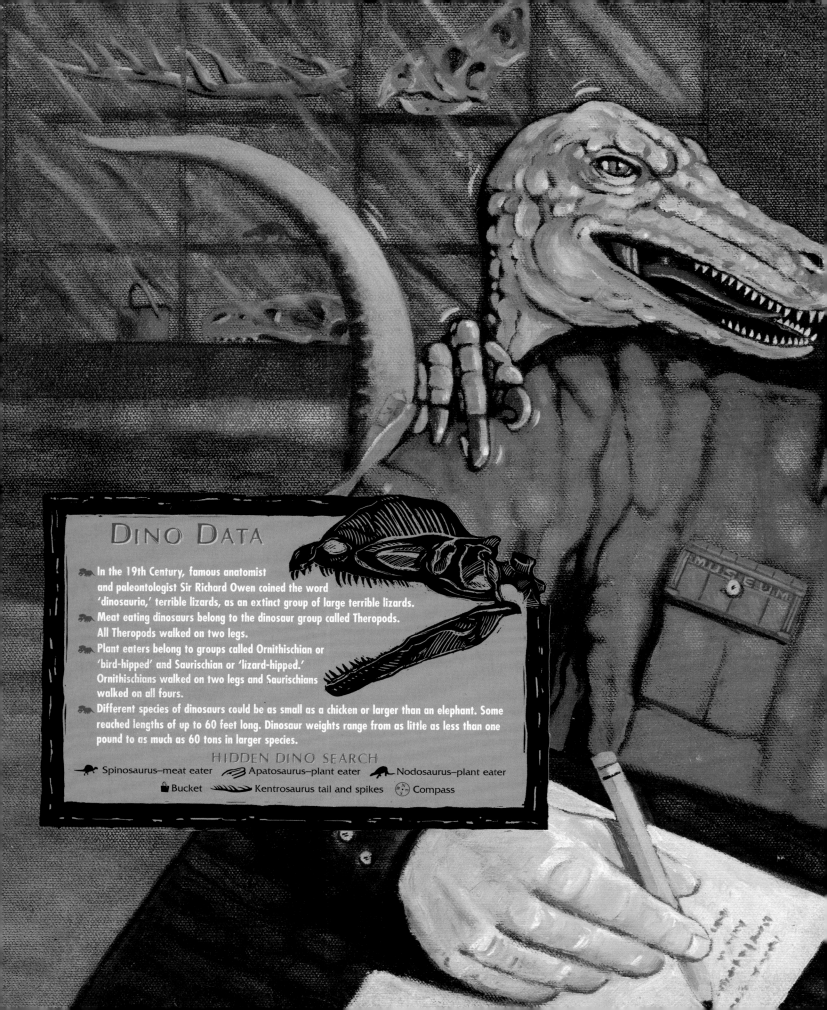

DINO DATA

- In the 19th Century, famous anatomist and paleontologist Sir Richard Owen coined the word 'dinosauria,' terrible lizards, as an extinct group of large terrible lizards.
- Meat eating dinosaurs belong to the dinosaur group called Theropods. All Theropods walked on two legs.
- Plant eaters belong to groups called Ornithischian or 'bird-hipped' and Saurischian or 'lizard-hipped.' Ornithischians walked on two legs and Saurischians walked on all fours.
- Different species of dinosaurs could be as small as a chicken or larger than an elephant. Some reached lengths of up to 60 feet long. Dinosaur weights range from as little as less than one pound to as much as 60 tons in larger species.

HIDDEN DINO SEARCH

Spinosaurus–meat eater   Apatosaurus–plant eater   Nodosaurus–plant eater

Bucket   Kentrosaurus tail and spikes   Compass

Skulls and tails and big spike plates.
Dino teeth, dino feet...let's measure their weight.

We'll go to work right here in the museum.
PaleoJoe puts the bones together and
you get to see 'em.

PaleoJoe is a paleontologist and he's Paleocool!
Maybe you too can go to paleontology school!

Dino Glossary

Aquatic — An animal or plant that lives in the water.

Carnivores — Animals that eat meat.

Cretaceous period — A first period of the age of dinosaurs from 145 to 65 million years ago.

Cropolites — Fossilized feces.

Defense — The ability or capability of an organism to protect itself or resisting attack.

Dinosaur — The general name derived from the Latin dinos meaning terrible and sauros meaning lizard. The name was originated by Sir Richard Owen of England.

Evidence — An indication of something that provides proof.

Fossils — The ancient remains of plants or animals that have turned into stone or evidence that such life existed.

Hadrosaurids — This is a name for all dinosaurs that had a mouth shaped similarly to a duck-bill.

Herbivore — An animal that exclusively ate plants.

Igneous — A type of rock formed by the volcanic action of the earth. Fossils are not found in this rock.

Jurassic period — The second period of the age of dinosaurs from 200 to 145 million years ago.

Legendary — An object or event of historical importance that became well known.

Meat eater — An animal that exclusively ate meat.

Metamorphic — Rock formed by the heat and pressure of the earth. Sometimes fossils are found in this rock.

Museum — An institution dedicated to the preservation, study, and display of something.

Paleontologist — A person who studies fossils.

Plant eater — An animal that ate plants, also called an herbivore.

Prehistoric — The time before humans began to record time and events.

Preserved — Something that was protected in order that it might be found later.

Primitive — Related to the earliest age or period.

Primitive feathers — Feathers of early dinosaurs. They resemble hollow quills. Some looked similar to the feathers of baby birds. These feathers could not be used to fly. They are believed to be for protection from heat or cold.

Reconstruct — To rebuild something the way it originally appeared.

Rhizoliths — Fossilized remains of primitive plant and tree roots.

Sedimentary — Rock formed in layers due to the weathering of the Earth's surface. Fossils are found in this type of rock.

Solar Science — The study of solar energy, which is energy obtained from radiation emitted by the sun.

Trace fossils — Preserved indirect evidence that a plant or animal existed.

Trackway — A trace fossil that shows evidence that an animal passed by. The preserved footprints of ancient animals.

Triassic period — The first period of the Age of Dinosaurs from 245 to 200 million years ago.

Timeline of the Age of Dinosaurs

Triassic period   245 – 200 million years ago
Jurassic period   200 – 145 million years ago
Cretaceous period 145 – 65 million years ago

PaleoJoe Treasures

Dinosaurs clomping and dinosaurs romping;
dinosaur feet stamping and loudly stomping.
Dinosaurs peeking and dinosaurs sleeping,
dinosaurs flying and dinosaurs leaping.

I hope you had fun on your dino adventures—
now you can find more hidden PaleoJoe Treasures.

 campfire

 campstool

 camp stove

 canteen

 coffee cup

 coil of rope

 coprolites (fossilized dinosaur poop)

 dental pick

 dinosaur egg and hatchling

 do-rag

 feather

 fossil fern

 glue

 goggles

 GPS unit

 Handkerchief

 Hidden Dinosaurs

 Insect repellent

 Kneepads

 Laptop computer

 Loupe

 Museum facade

 Paint brush

 Palette knife

 Petrified wood

 Pry bar

 Rib bone

 Roll of paper towel

 Safety glasses

 Satellite

 Seashell

 Sifting screen

 Sunglasses

 Sun shelter tarp

 Surveyor's flag

 Swiss army knife

 Tape measure

 Tool roll

 Tour guide

 Tripod

 Walkie talkie

Water bottle